My First Hungarian
Body Parts

Picture Book with English Translations

Published By: My First Picture Book™

Ever Wondered How That Word Sounds?

We've introduced complimentary audio recordings for all our books to enhance your reading experience. Dive into the sounds at **MyFirstPictureBook.com** and not only read, but also listen and learn.

A Heartfelt Message from Our Publishers:

Your support does more than just buy a book. It uplifts native authors and fuels the dreams of a close-knit business. We value every reader, and your insights could shape our next bestseller! Got suggestions or feedback? Let's co-create magic. Connect with us through the 'Contact Us' section on our website at **MyFirstPictureBook.com**.

Ankle

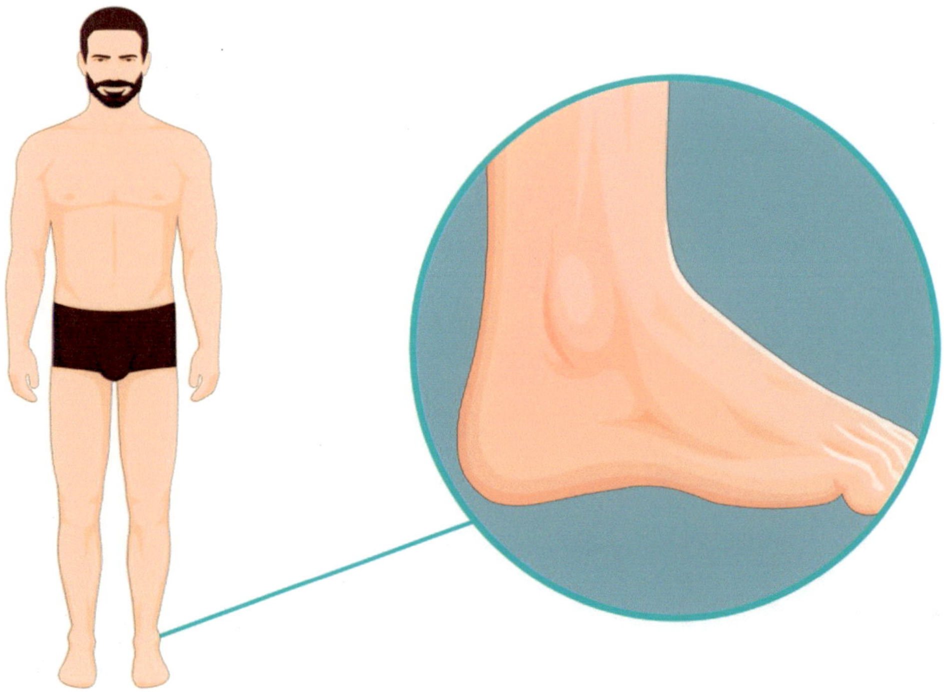

boka

boh-kah

Arm

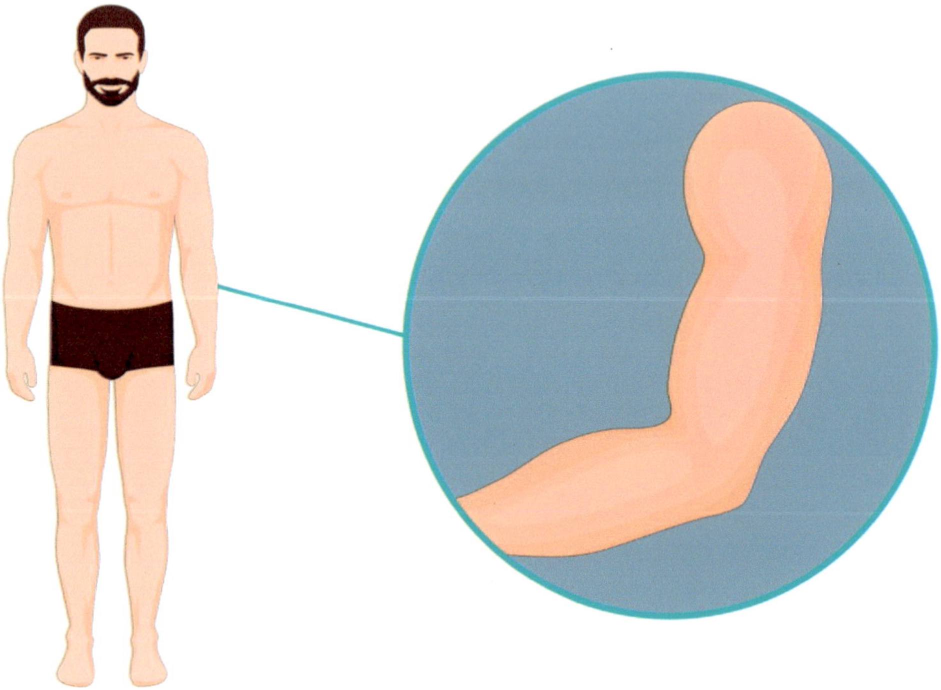

kar

kar

Back

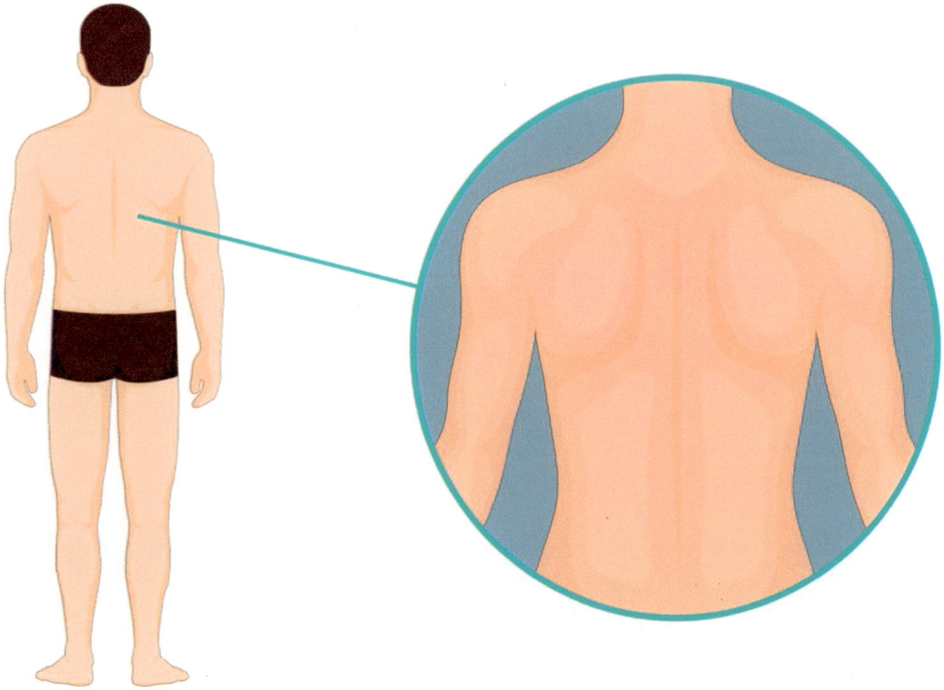

hát

haht

Beard

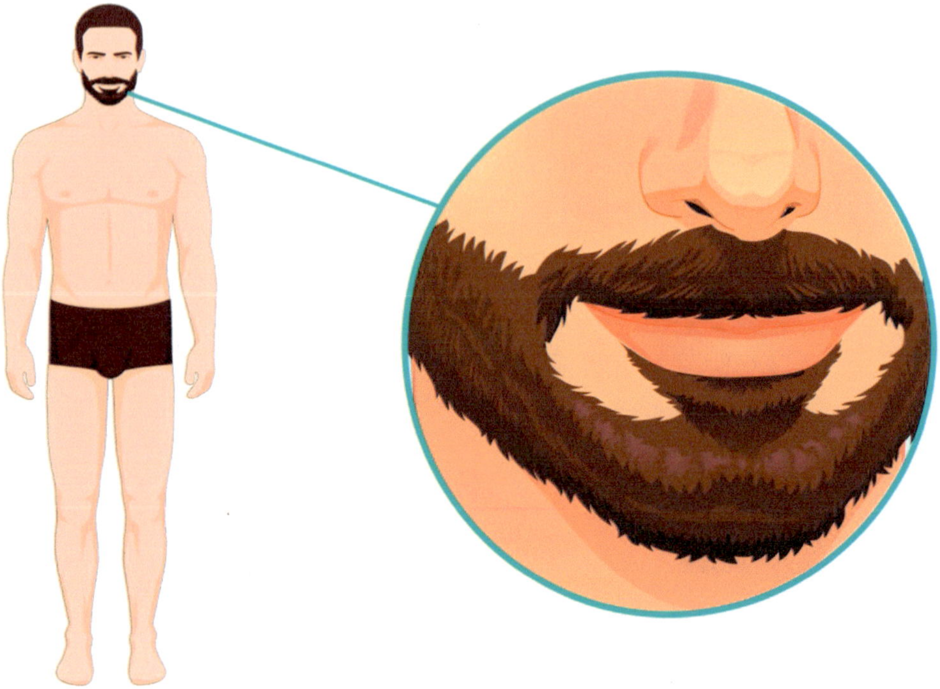

szakáll

soh-kahl

Brain

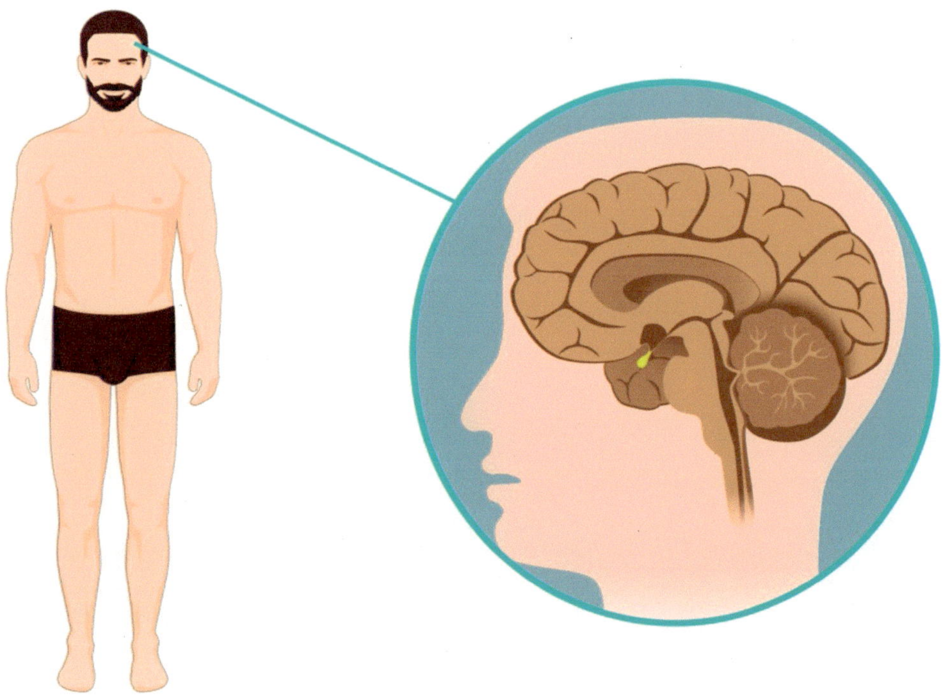

agy

ohd

Chin

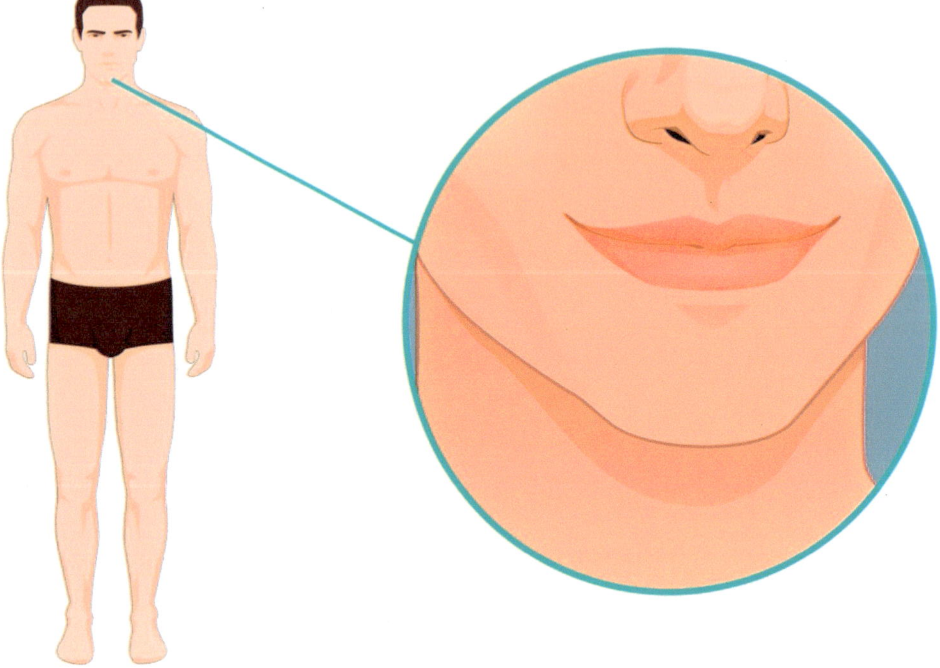

áll

ahl

Ear

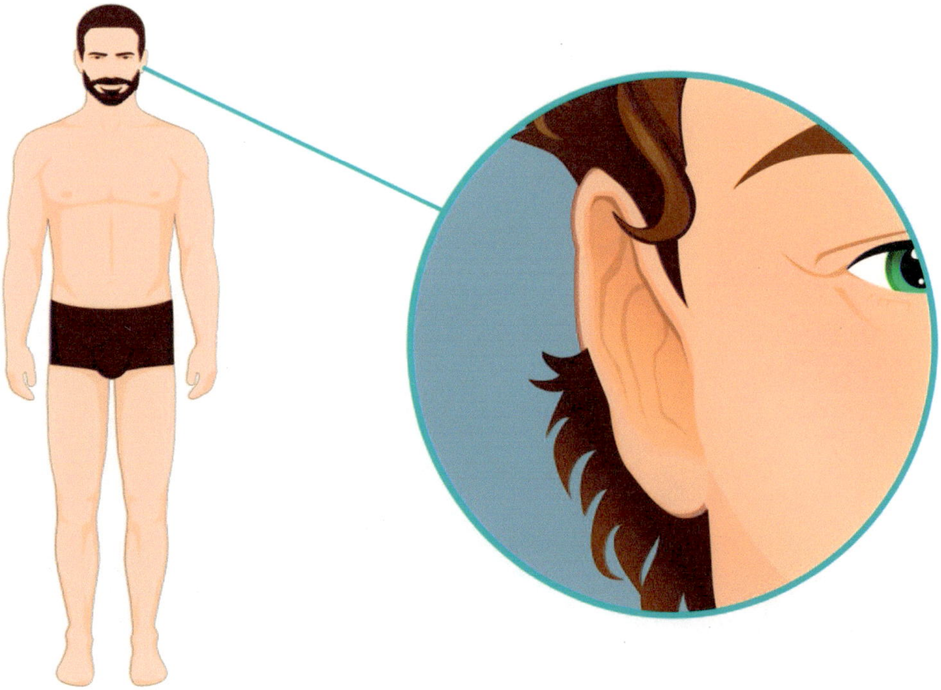

fül

fuul

Elbow

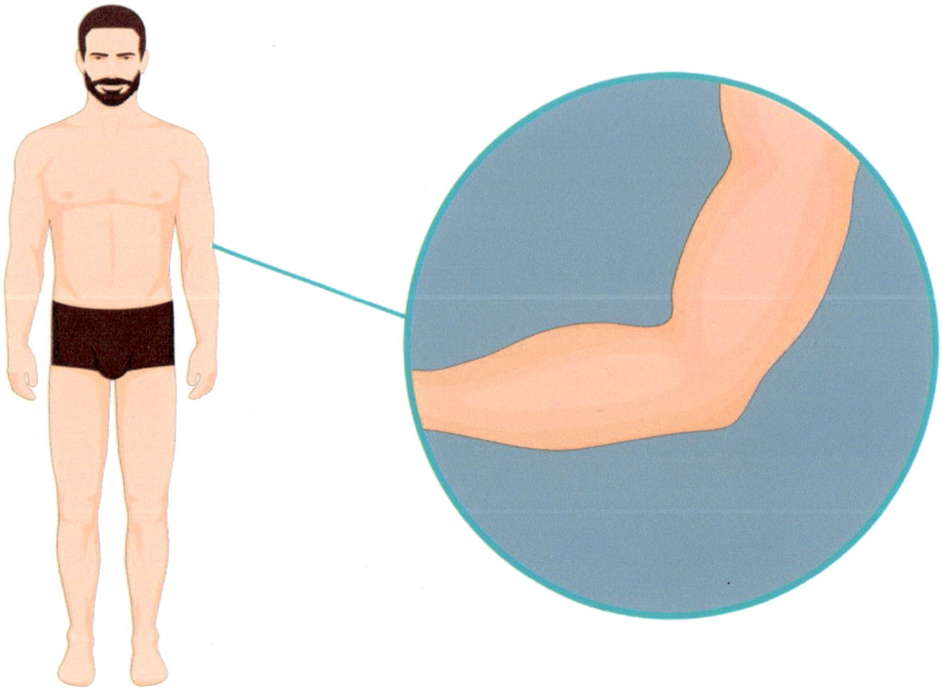

könyök

koen-yuk

Eye

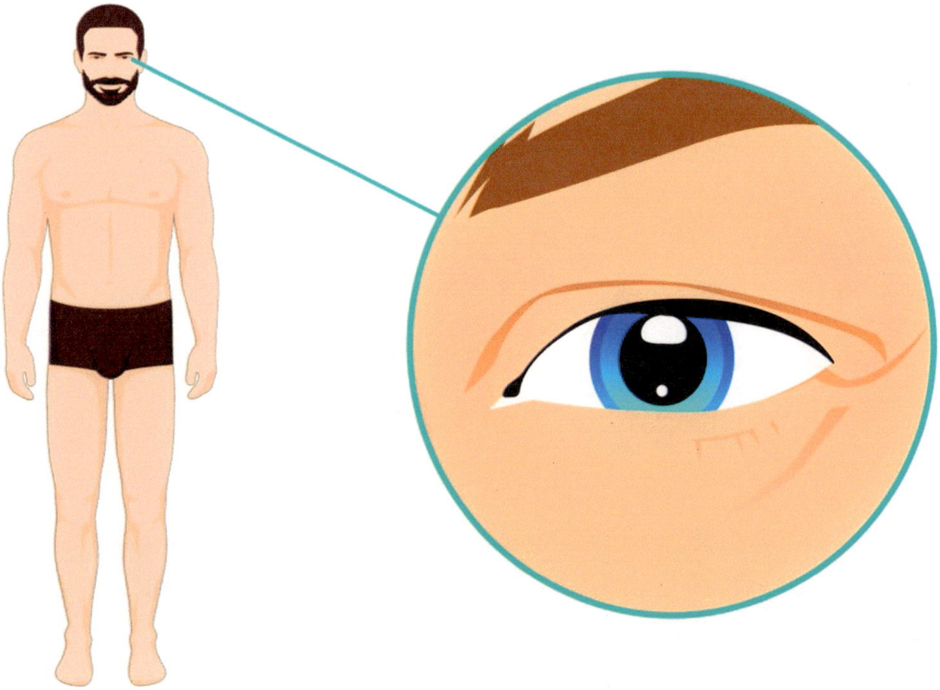

szem

sem

Eyebrow

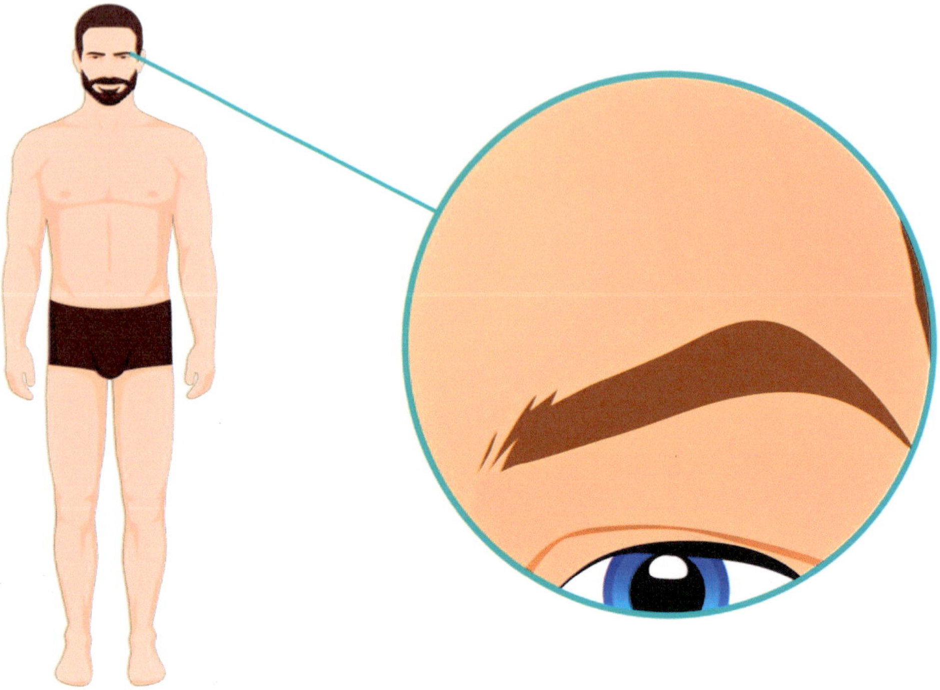

szemöldök

sem-oldoek

Face

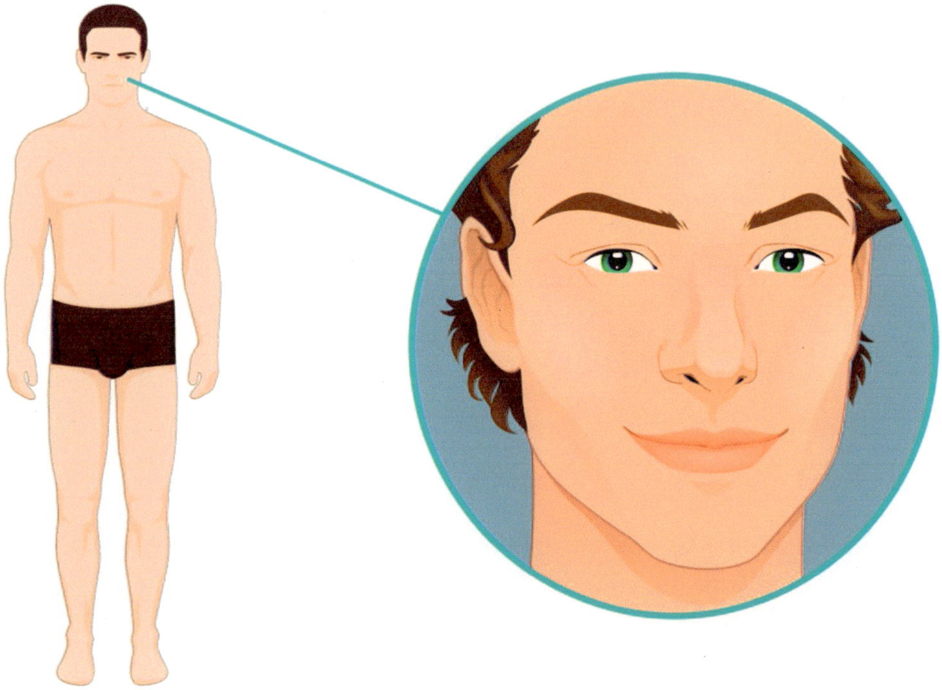

arc

arts

Finger

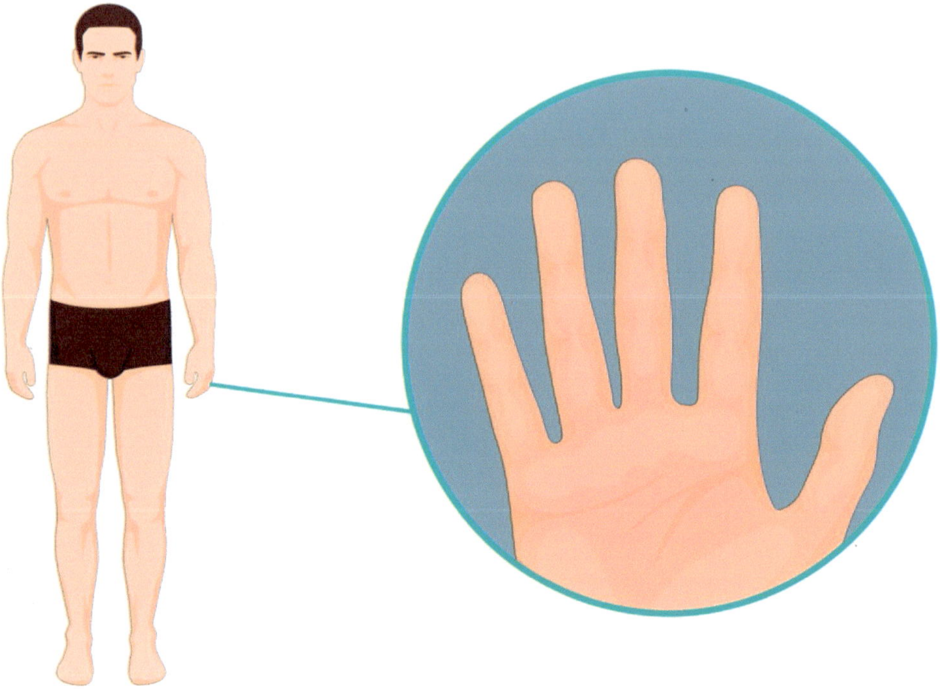

ujj

uy

Forehead

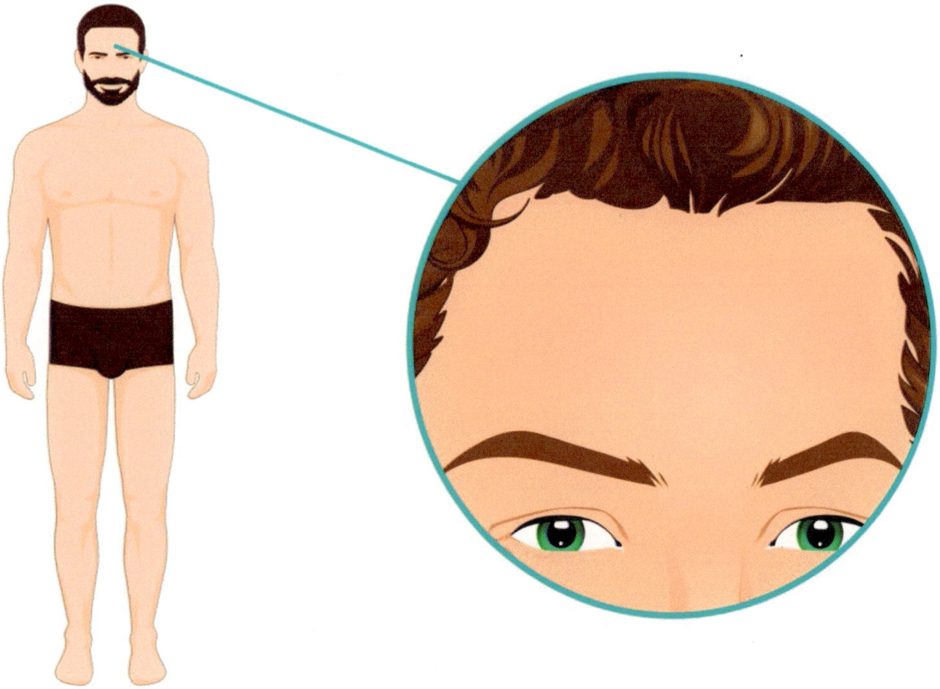

homlok

home-lok

Hair

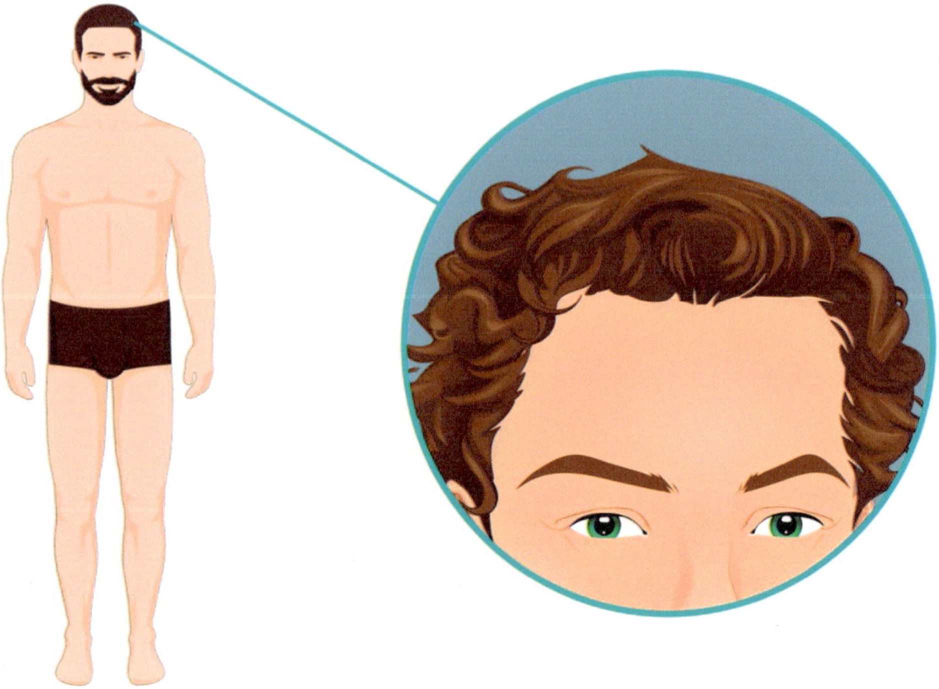

haj

hohy

Hand

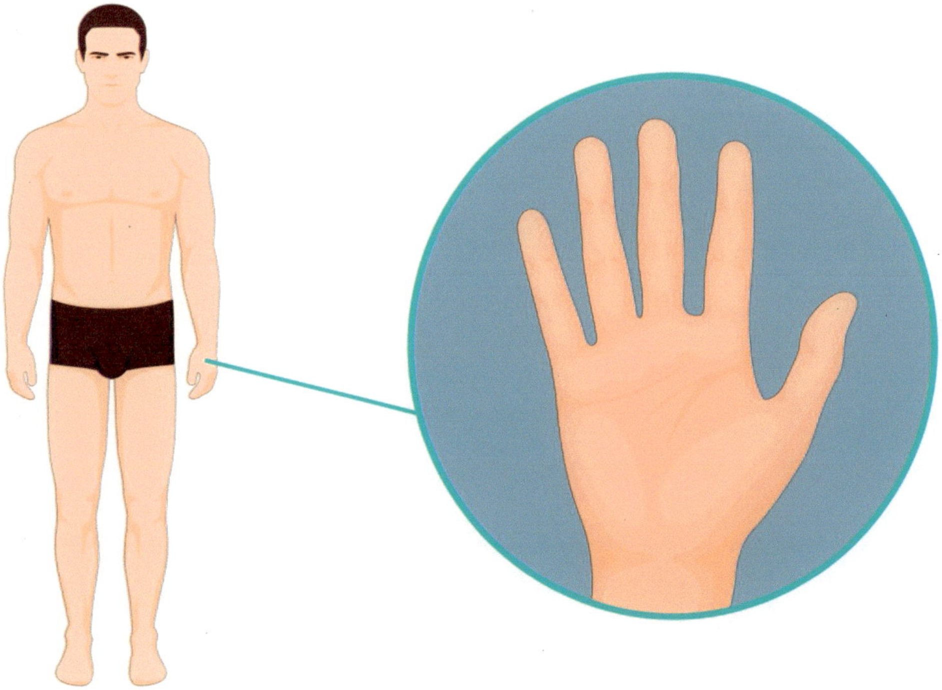

kéz

kez

Head

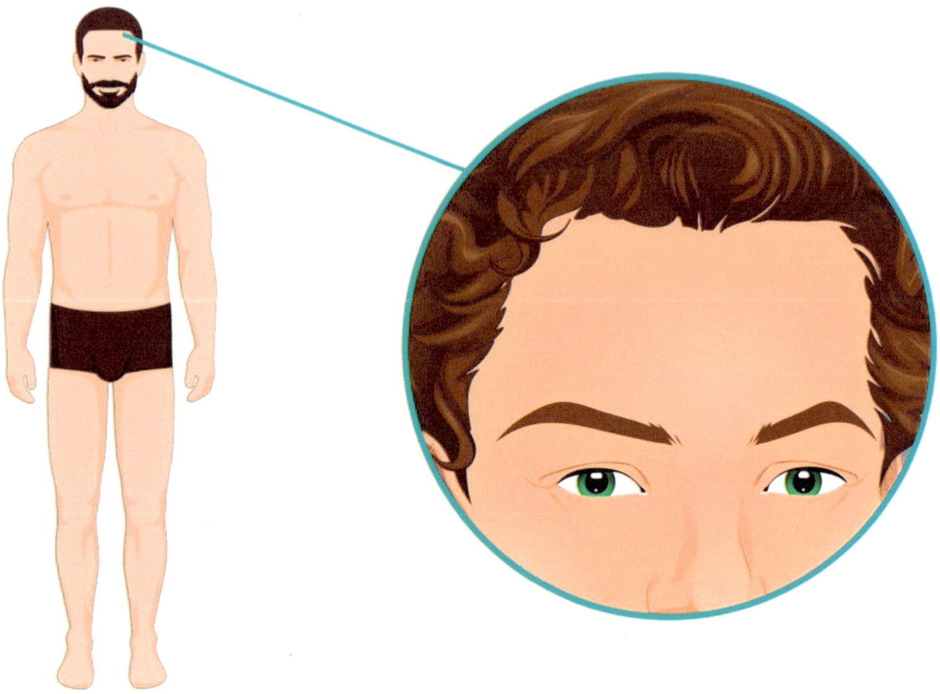

fej

fay

Heart

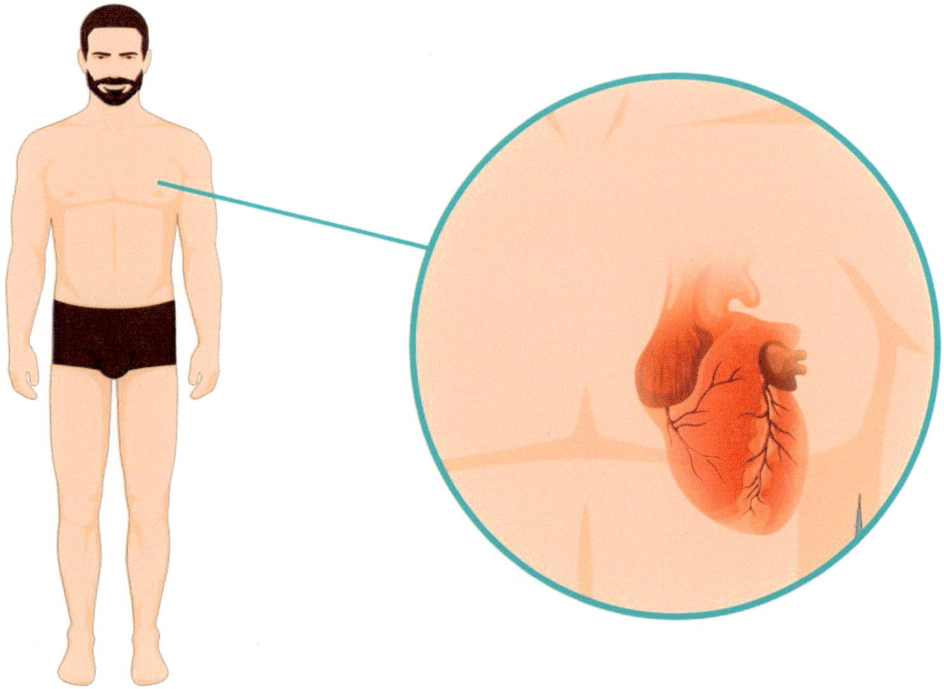

szív

seev

Heel

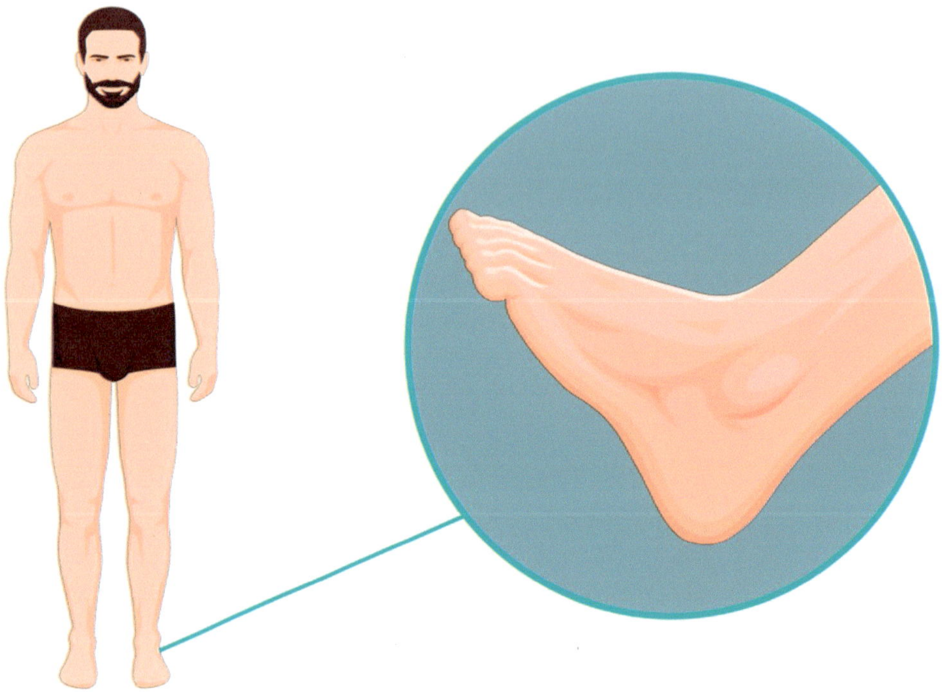

sarok

shah-rok

Knee

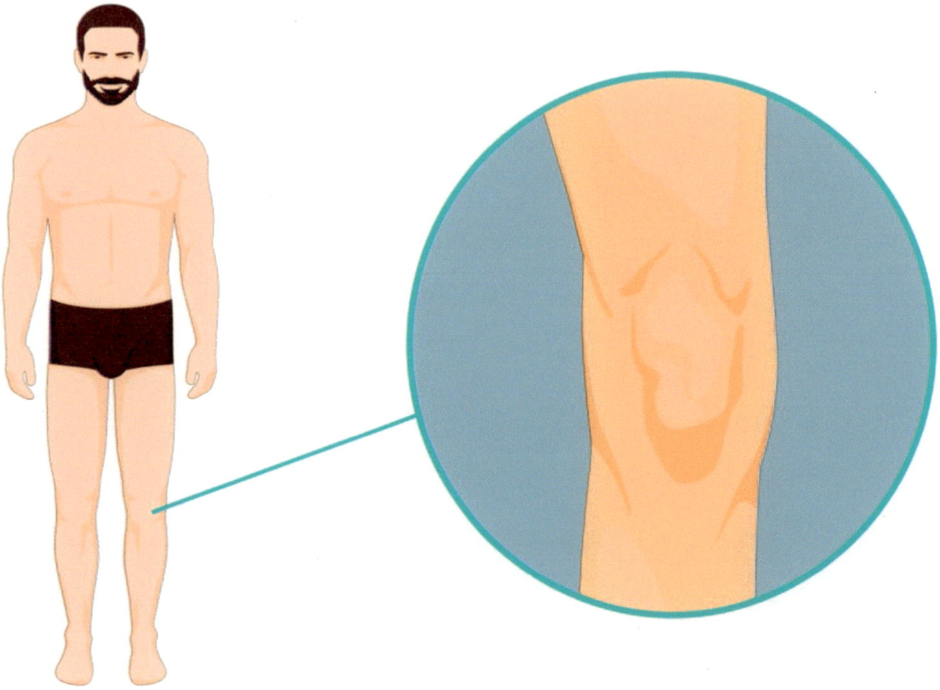

térd

teyrd

Leg

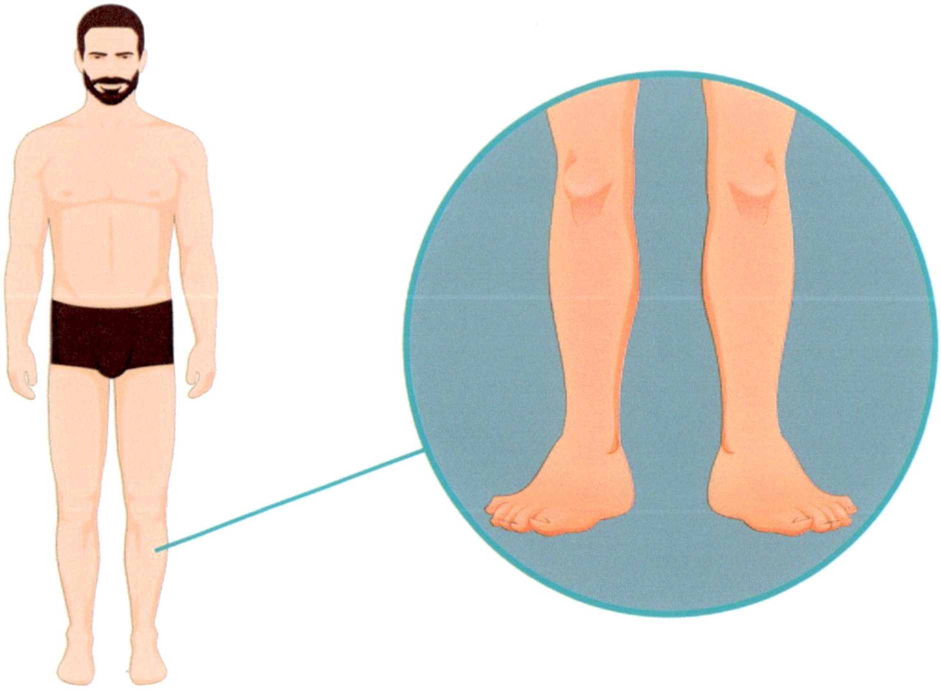

láb

lahr

Lip

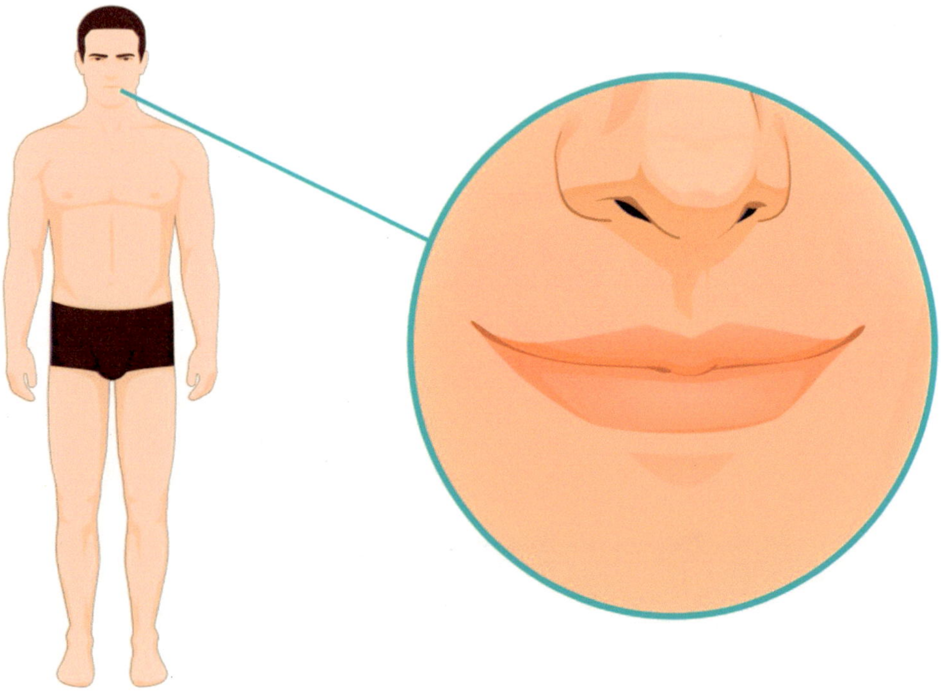

ajak

aw-yahk

Lung

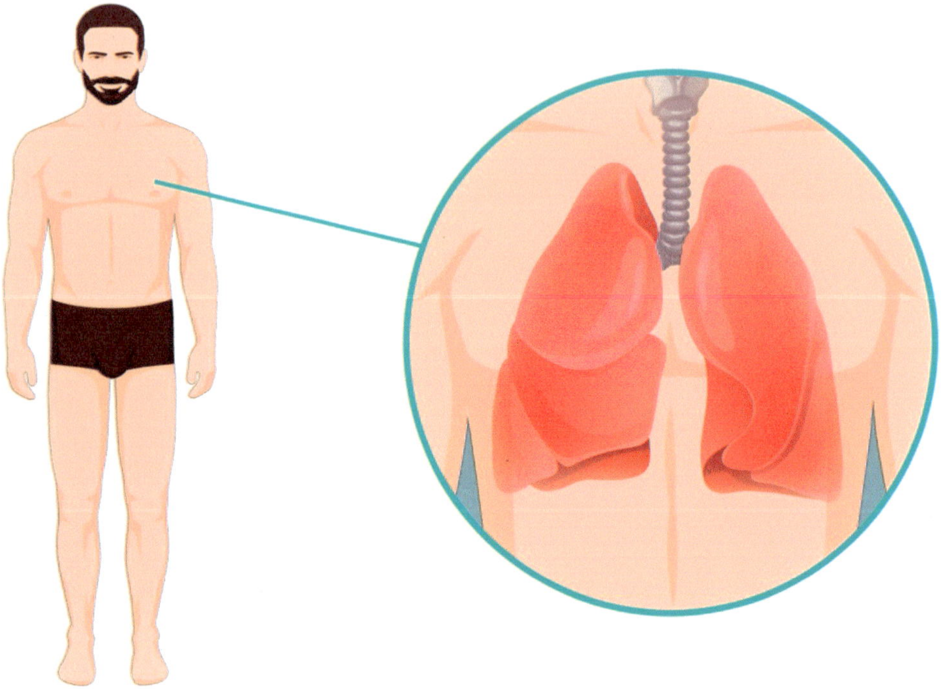

tüdő

too-duh

Moustache

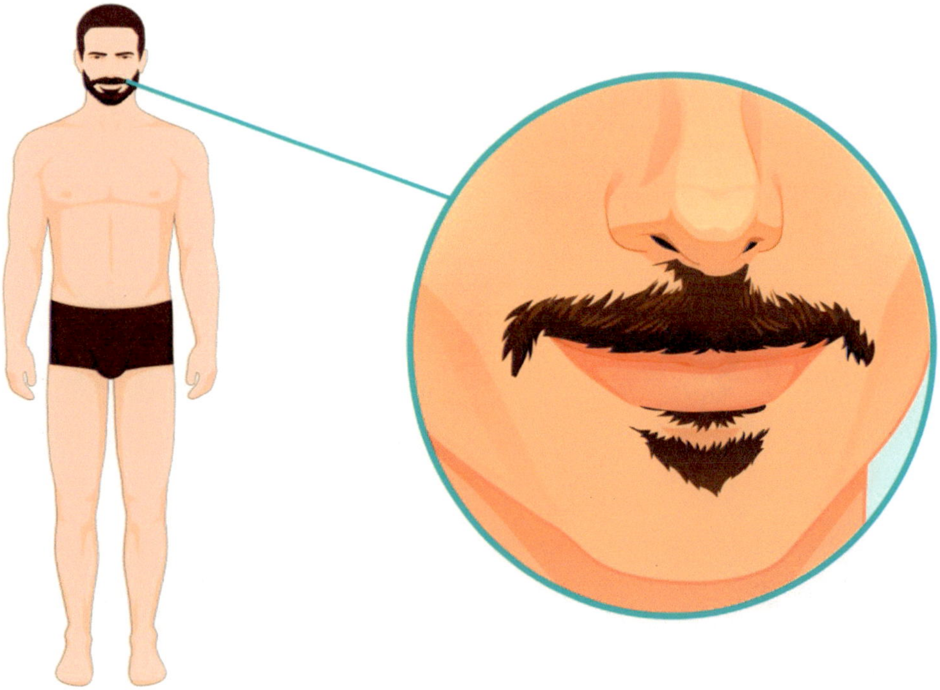

bajusz

bah-yus

Mouth

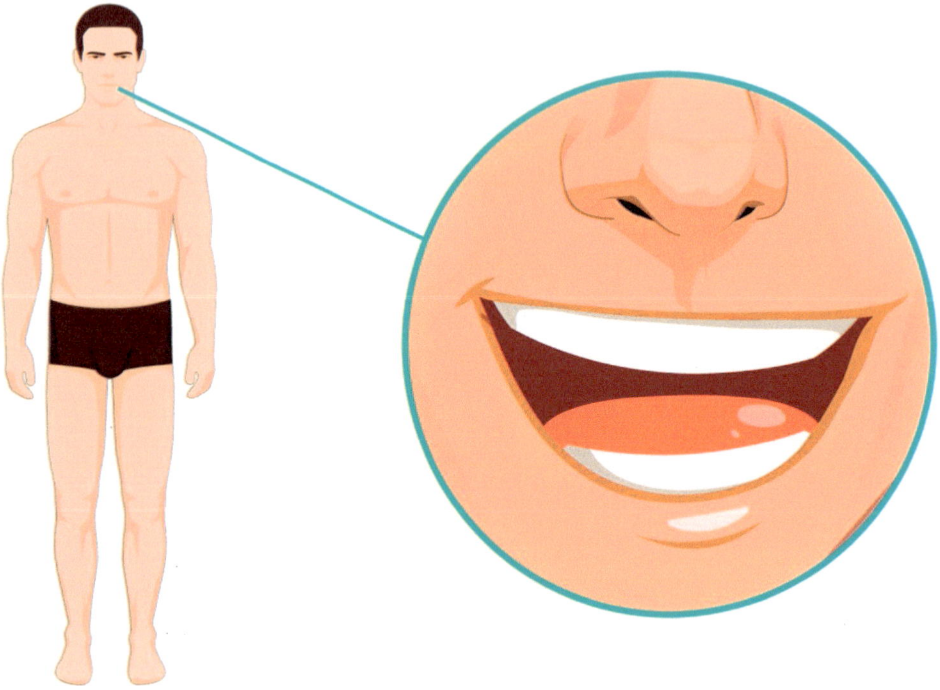

száj

sah-y

Nail

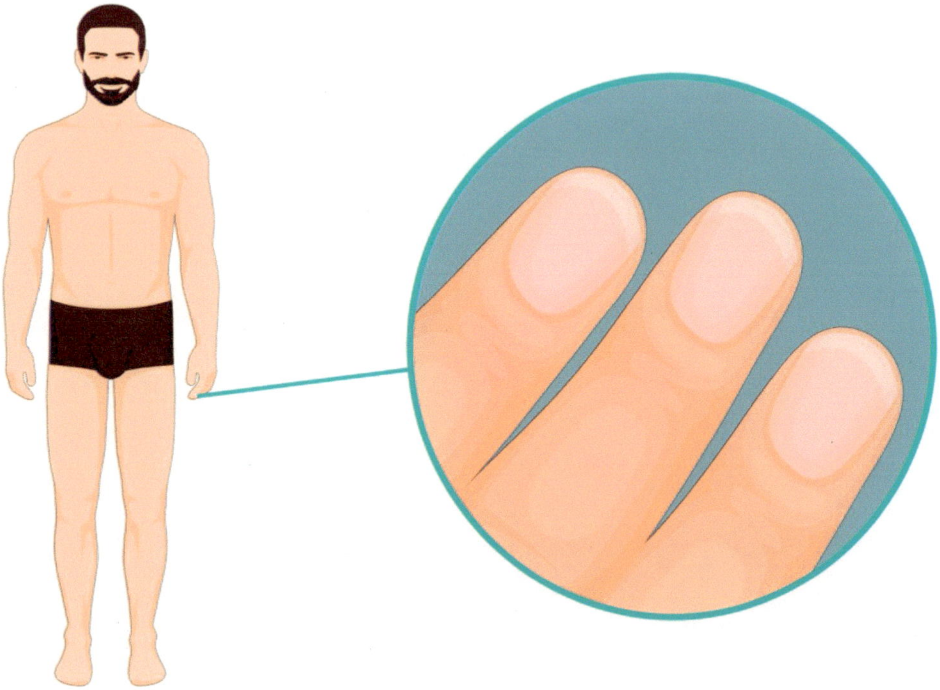

köröm

koe-ruhm

Neck

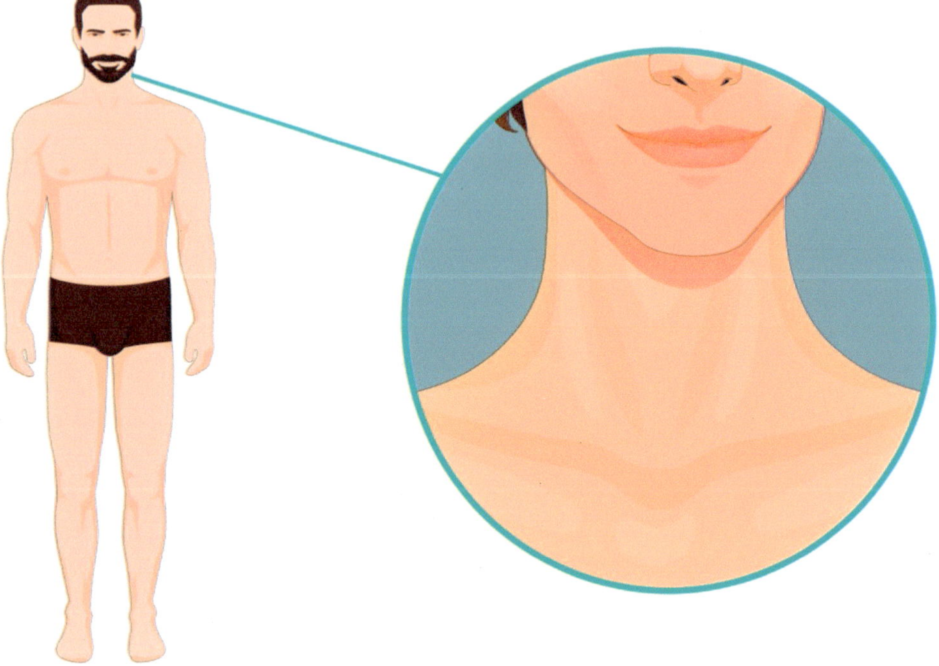

nyak

nyahk

Nose

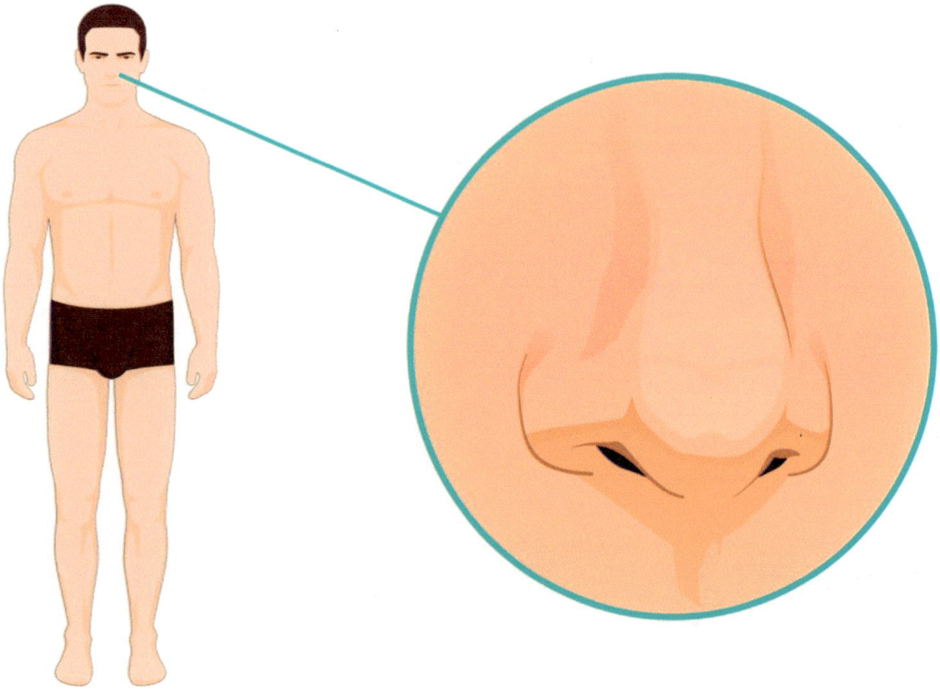

orr

or

Shoulder

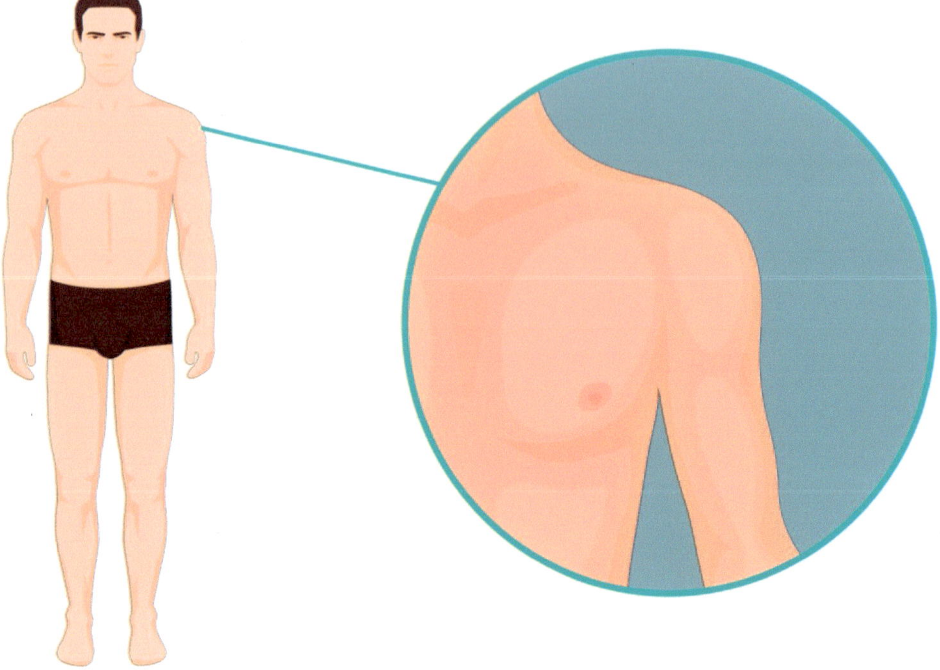

váll

vahl

Skin

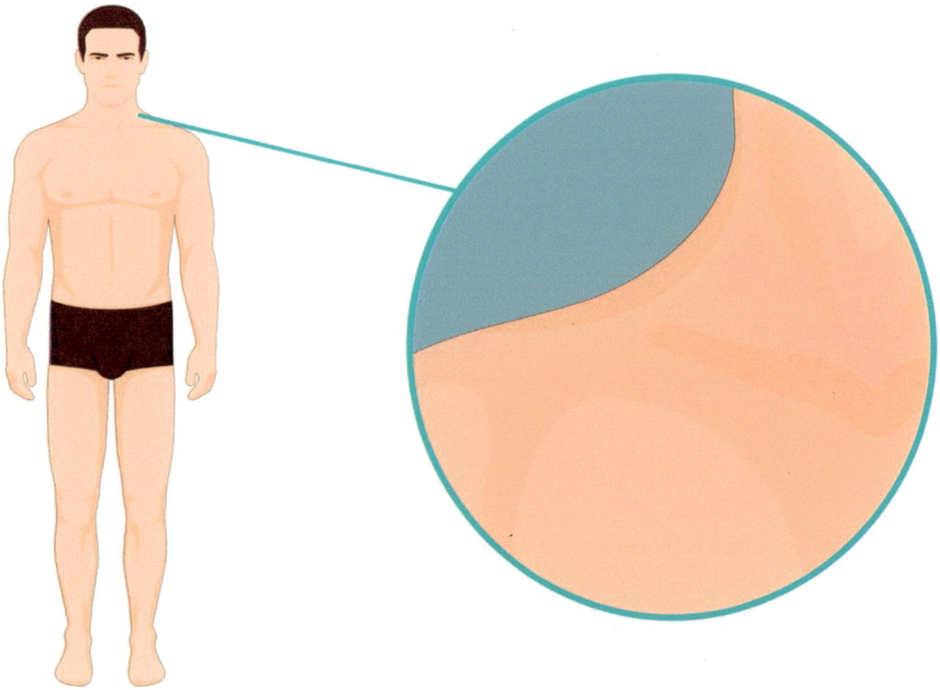

bőr

bur

Stomach

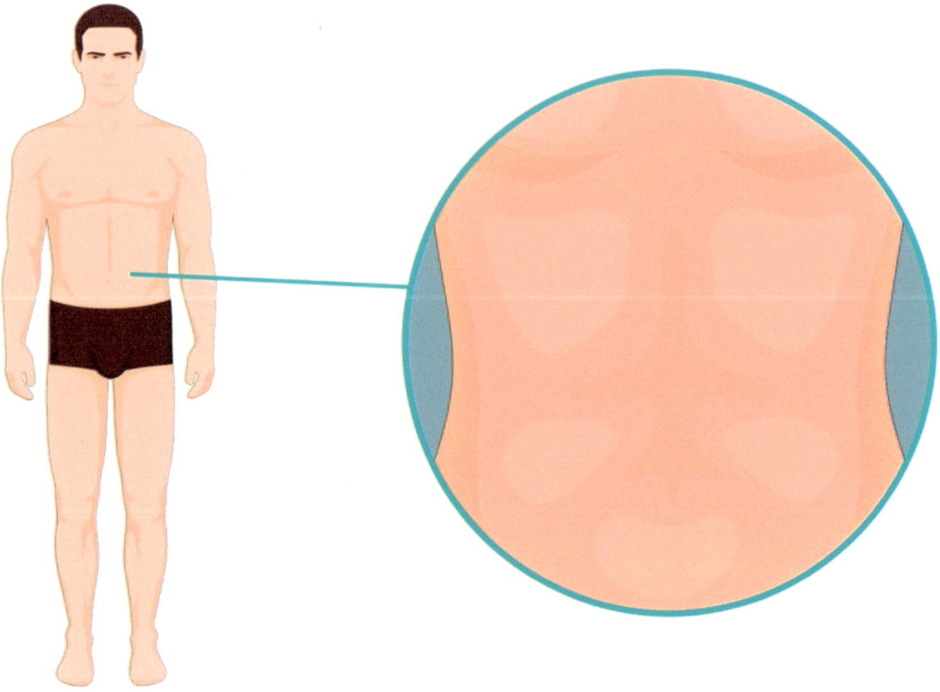

gyomor

yuh-mor

Thumb

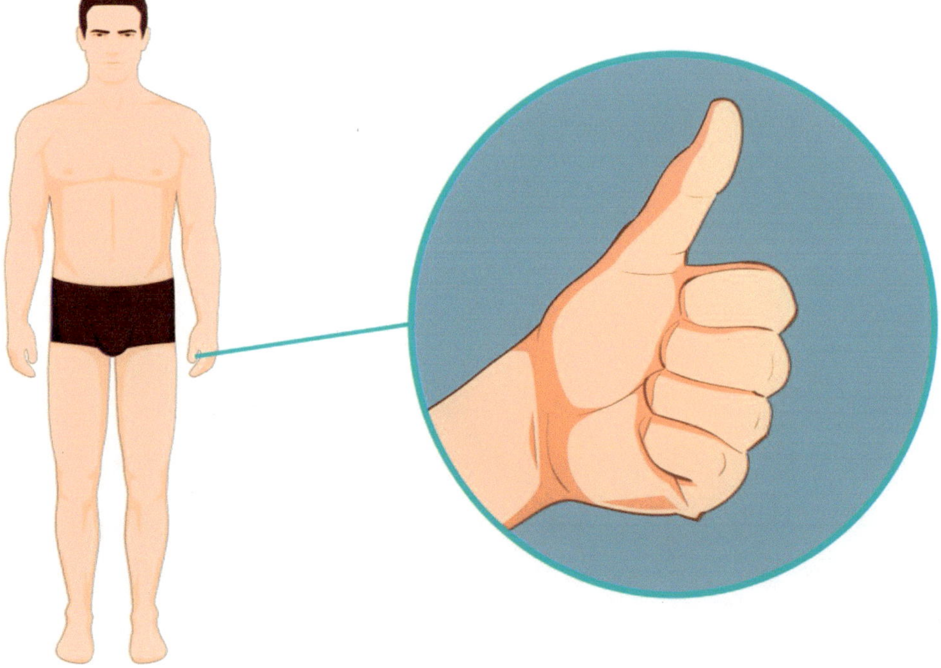

huvelykujj

hoo-vey-koo-yee

Toe

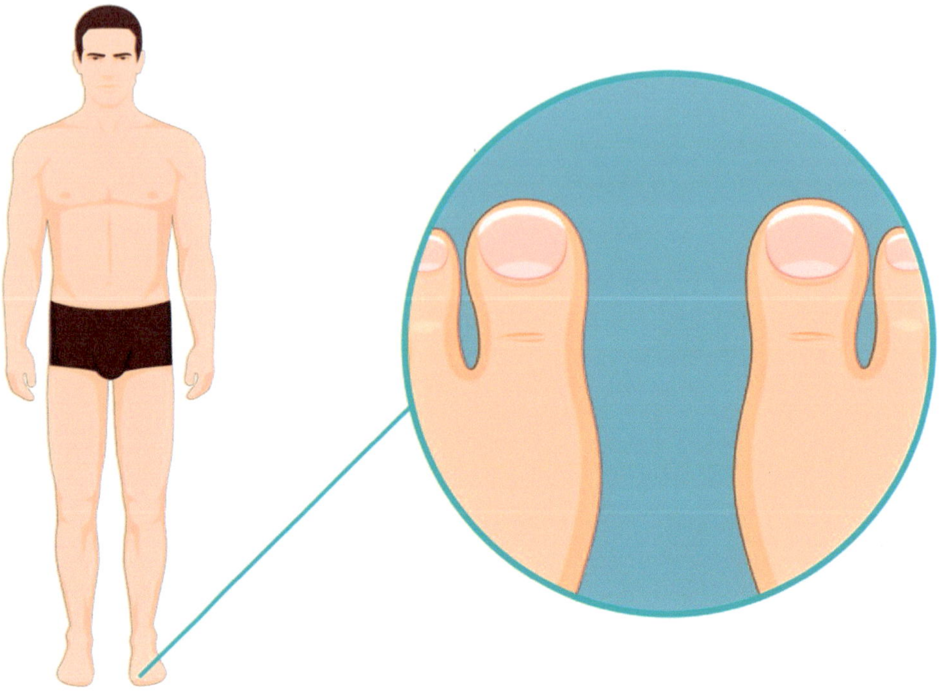

lábujj

lah-booy

Tongue

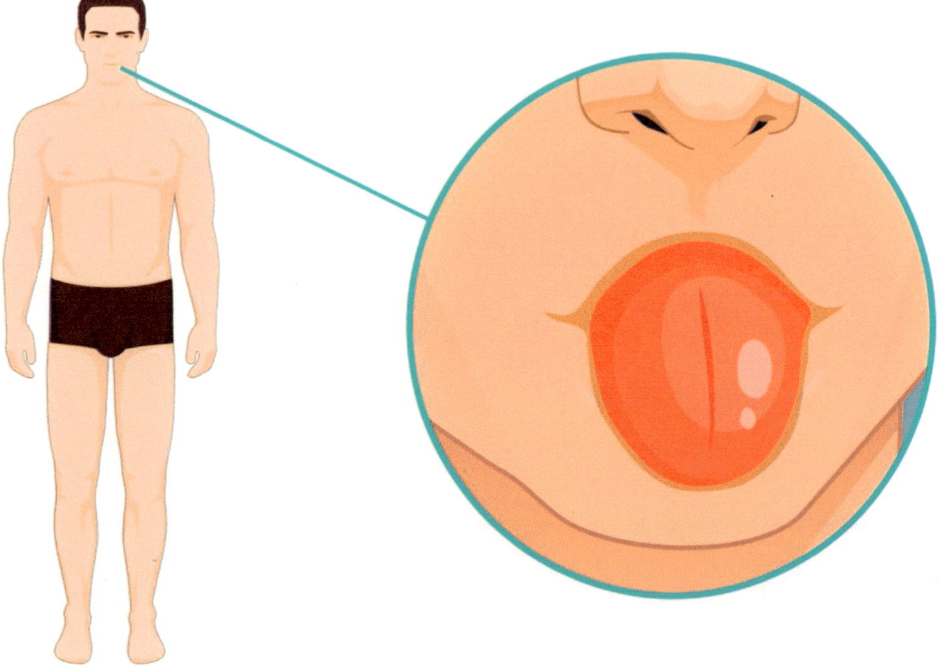

nyelv

ny-elv

Tooth

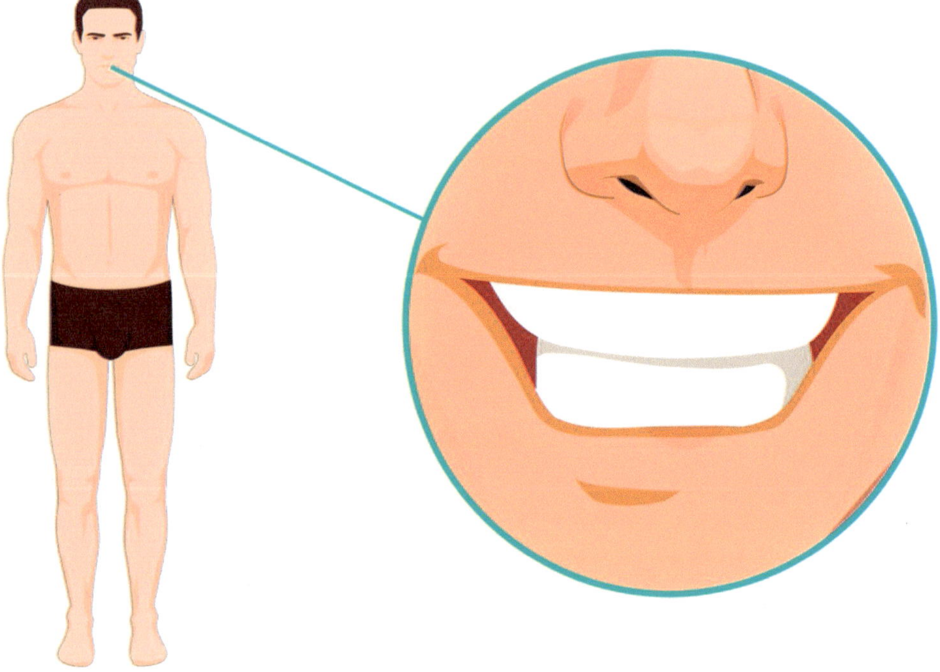

fog

fog

Wrist

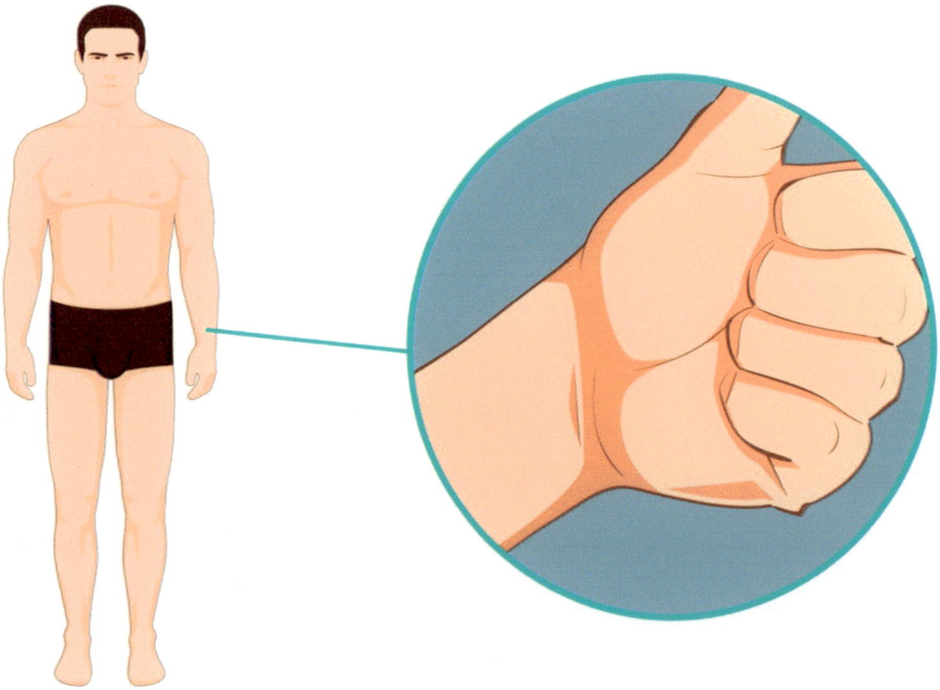

csukló

choo-kloh

Made in the USA
Monee, IL
05 November 2026

67375721R00024